From the movie

Disney

FROZEN

COOL COLOURING

PaRragon

Bath • New York • Singapore • Hong Kong • Cologne • Delhi
Melbourne • Amsterdam • Johannesburg • Shenzhen

Elsa has magical powers, to create ice and snow.
One night, she accidentally hits her little sister, Anna, with an icy blast.
Their parents, the king and queen, are worried.

The sisters grow apart as they get older.

When the sisters are grown up, Princess Anna meets Prince Hans at Elsa's coronation. They quickly fall in love and get engaged.

Queen Elsa doesn't approve of Anna's quick engagement to Hans.

Elsa gets upset when she argues with her sister
and accidentally blasts ice in front of everyone. She runs away from
Arendelle and, as she leaves, snow and ice cover the ground.

Anna decides to go after Elsa. She asks Hans
to take care of the kingdom while she is away.

Once she is alone, Elsa is finally free to use her powers. She builds a stunning ice palace.

Elsa practises her icy powers.

Princess Anna rides her horse through
the winter storm in the mountains.

Anna is thrown from her horse and lands in the snow.
Luckily she finds shelter in a remote shop.

Anna meets a snow-covered Kristoff inside the small shop.
He's not happy about the winter storm!

Oaken is the owner of the shop and sells supplies to travellers.

Kristoff's best friend is a reindeer called Sven.

Anna asks Kristoff to take her to Elsa.
To help persuade him, she gives Sven carrots.

Anna, Kristoff and Sven find Elsa's icy wonderland –
and a walking, talking snowman called Olaf!

Olaf is a magical snowman who likes warm hugs.

When Anna finds Elsa, she asks her sister to return to Arendelle.
Elsa doesn't want to go back and the sisters argue.

Although she doesn't mean to, Elsa hits Anna in the chest with
a blast of ice because she can't control her powers when she is upset.

Elsa creates a giant snowman called Marshmallow!

Marshmallow runs after Anna and Kristoff,
who run down the mountain.

Anna learns that the blast of ice from Elsa is freezing her heart – only an act of true love can thaw a frozen heart. Kristoff rushes Anna back to Hans.

Meanwhile, Hans goes to look for Anna and arrives at the ice palace.
He asks Elsa to return to Arendelle, but she doesn't want to.

Prince Hans returns to Arendelle to find Anna waiting for him but he refuses to kiss her.
He tells her that he never loved her and locks Anna away as she slowly freezes.

After leaving Anna at the kingdom gates Kristoff heads back to the mountains, but Sven wants Kristoff to return to Arendelle because he knows that Kristoff loves Anna.

Anna manages to escape from the castle but she is freezing to her core.
Kristoff runs to Anna – can he save her?

Anna makes a decision. She sees that her sister is in danger as Hans sneaks up behind Elsa. Anna needs to help her sister, but without Kristoff's kiss she will die.

Anna saves her sister by jumping in front of Elsa as Hans tries
to strike her with his sword. Anna turns to ice and the sword snaps.

Kristoff makes sure that Hans cannot strike a second blow.

Elsa hugs her sister and cries as she realizes that Anna saved her life.

But Anna's act of true love for her sister means that
the spell is broken and the ice melts.

Kristoff decides to stay in Arendelle with Anna!